Fantasy Faces

A coloring book for adults and all ages!

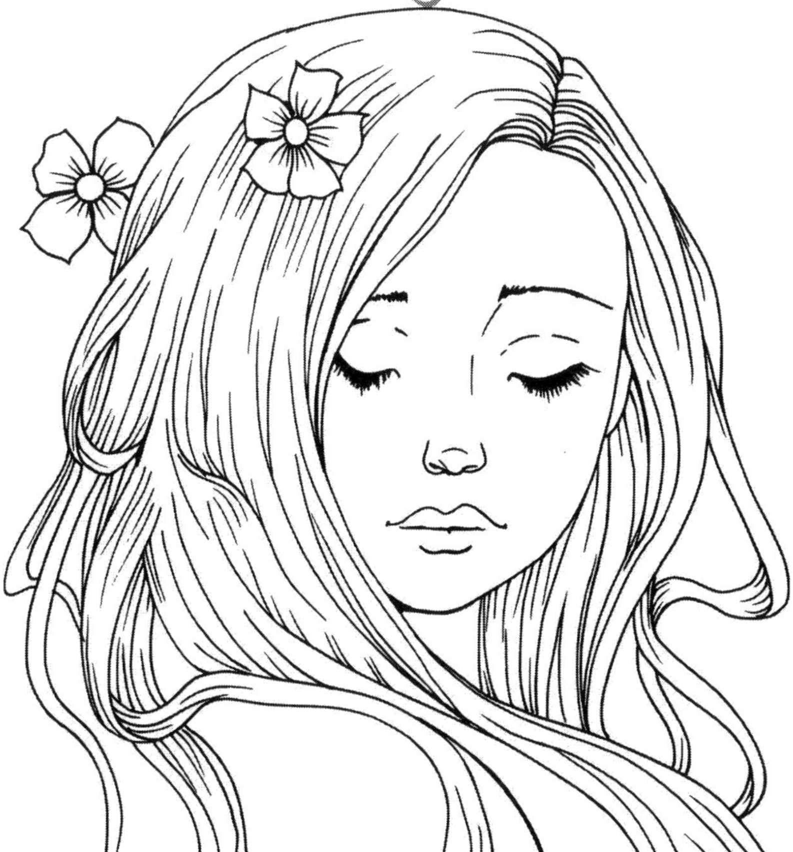

By Molly Harrison

www.mollyharrisonart.com

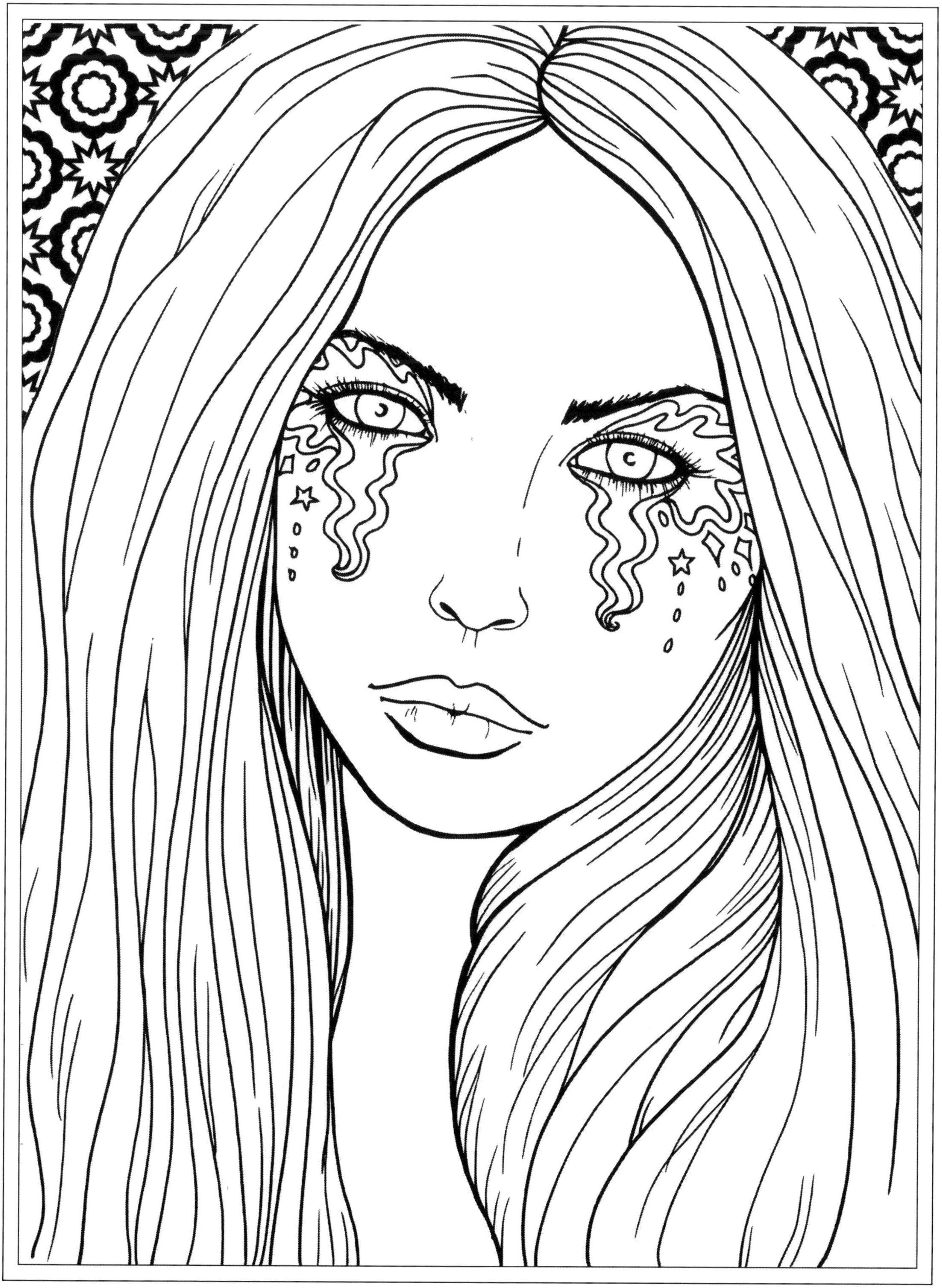

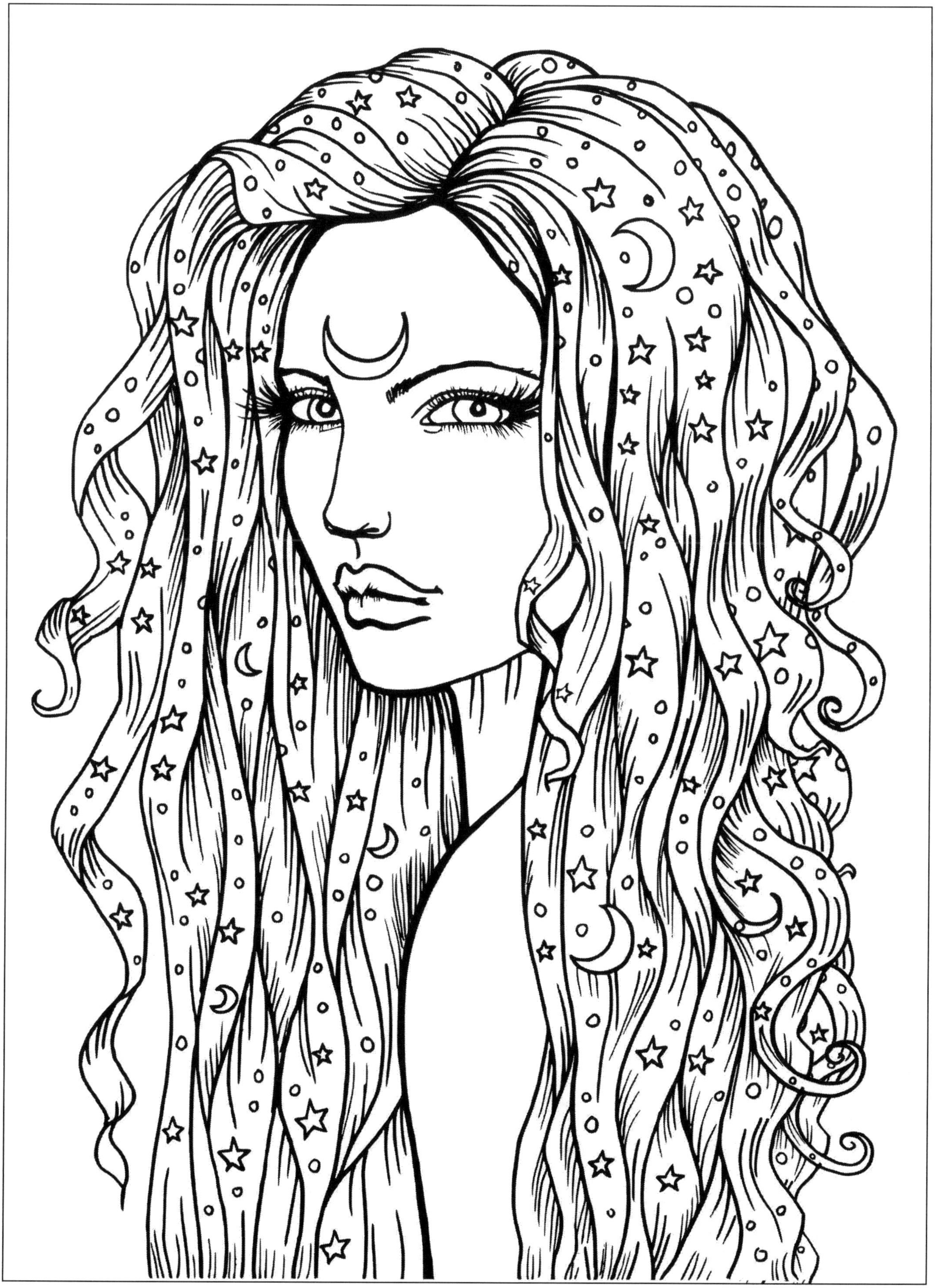

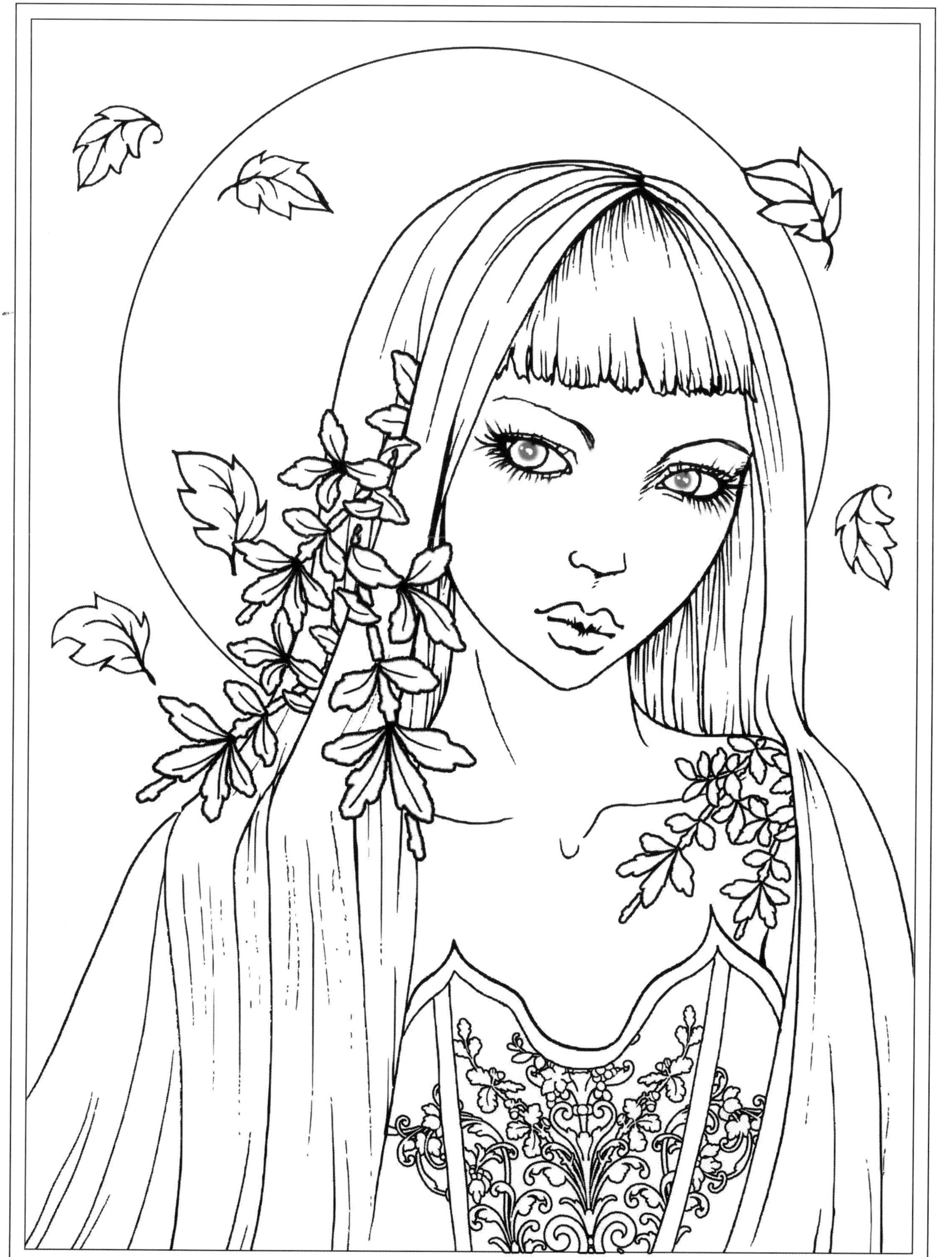

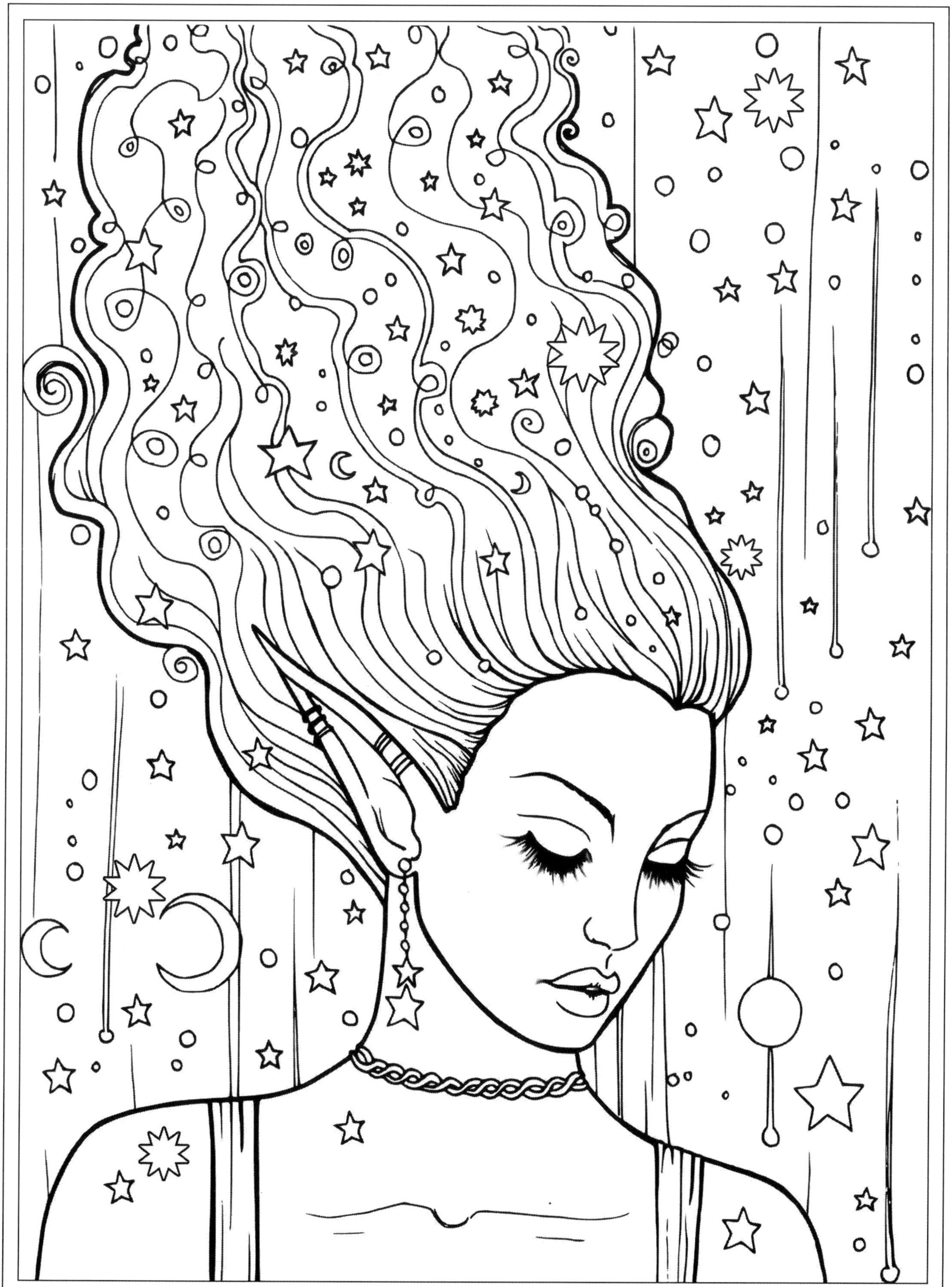

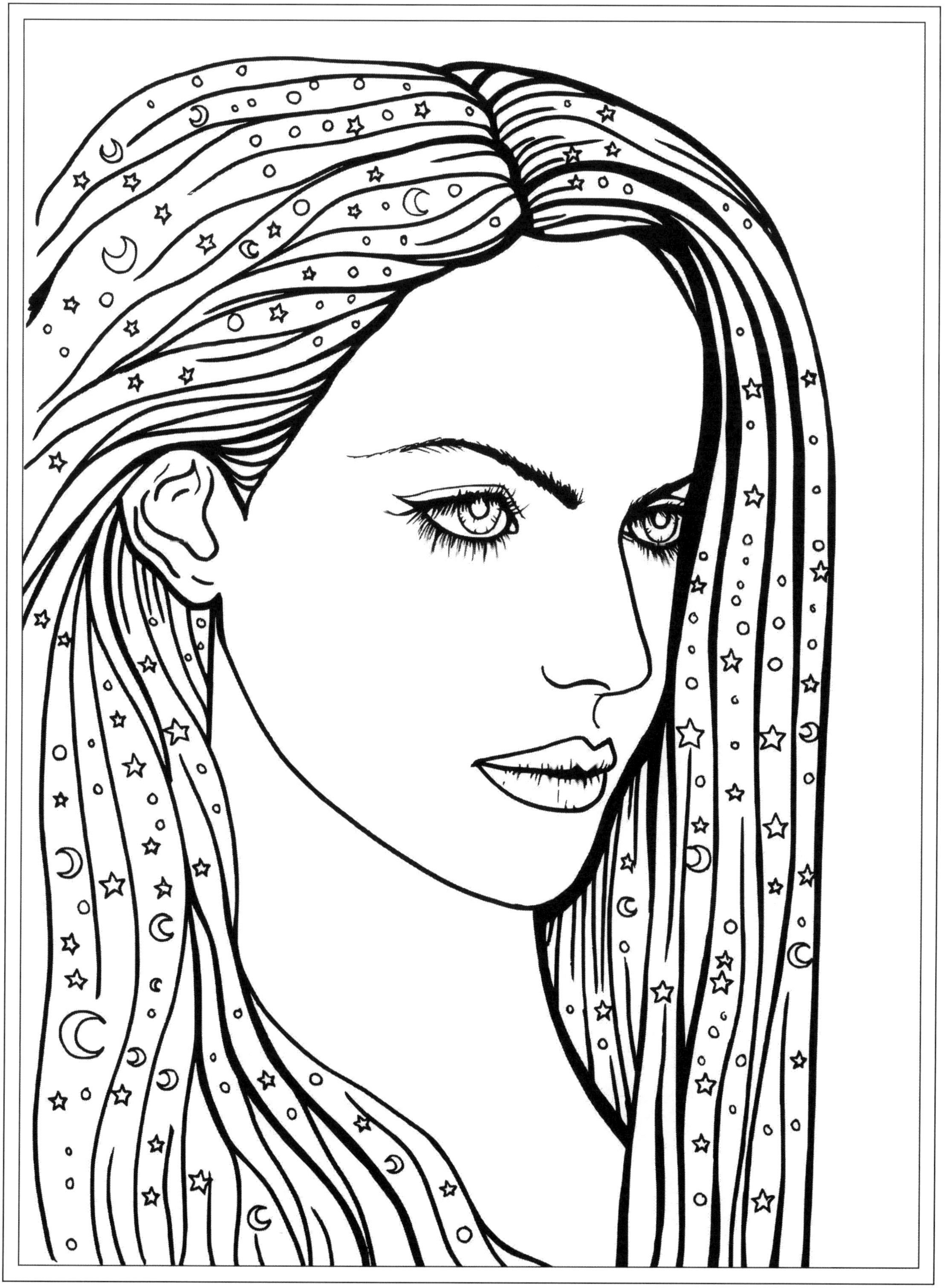

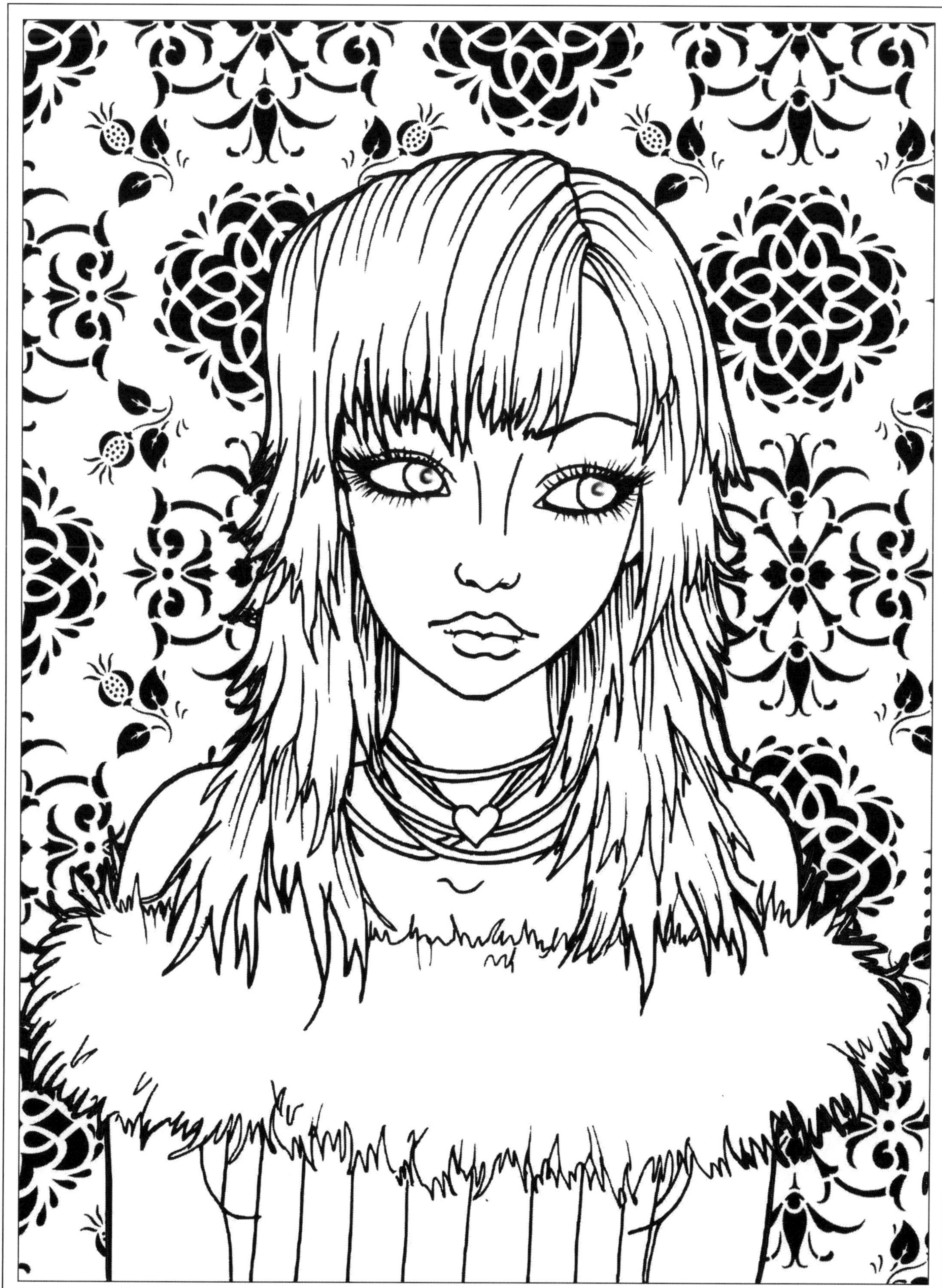

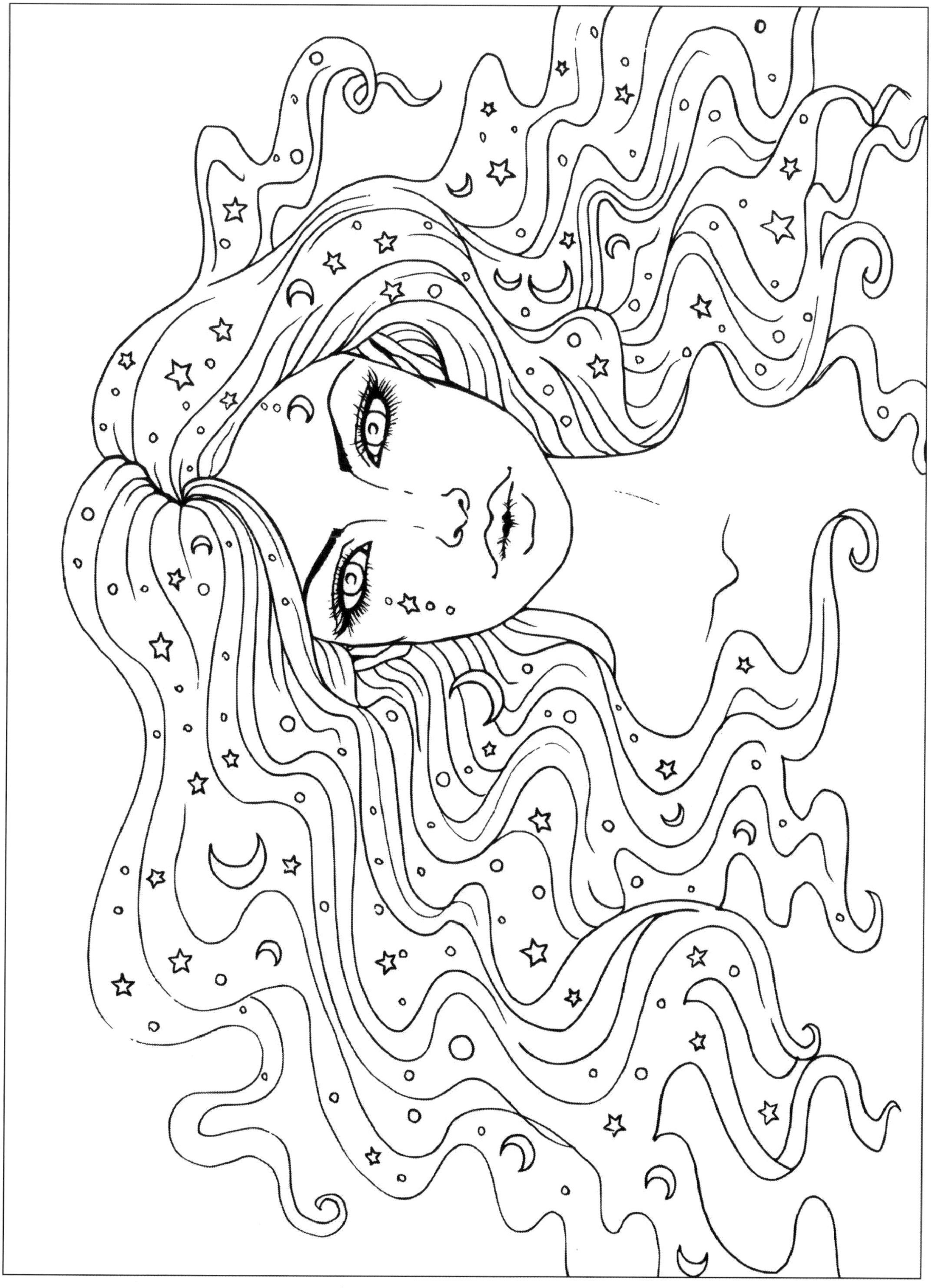

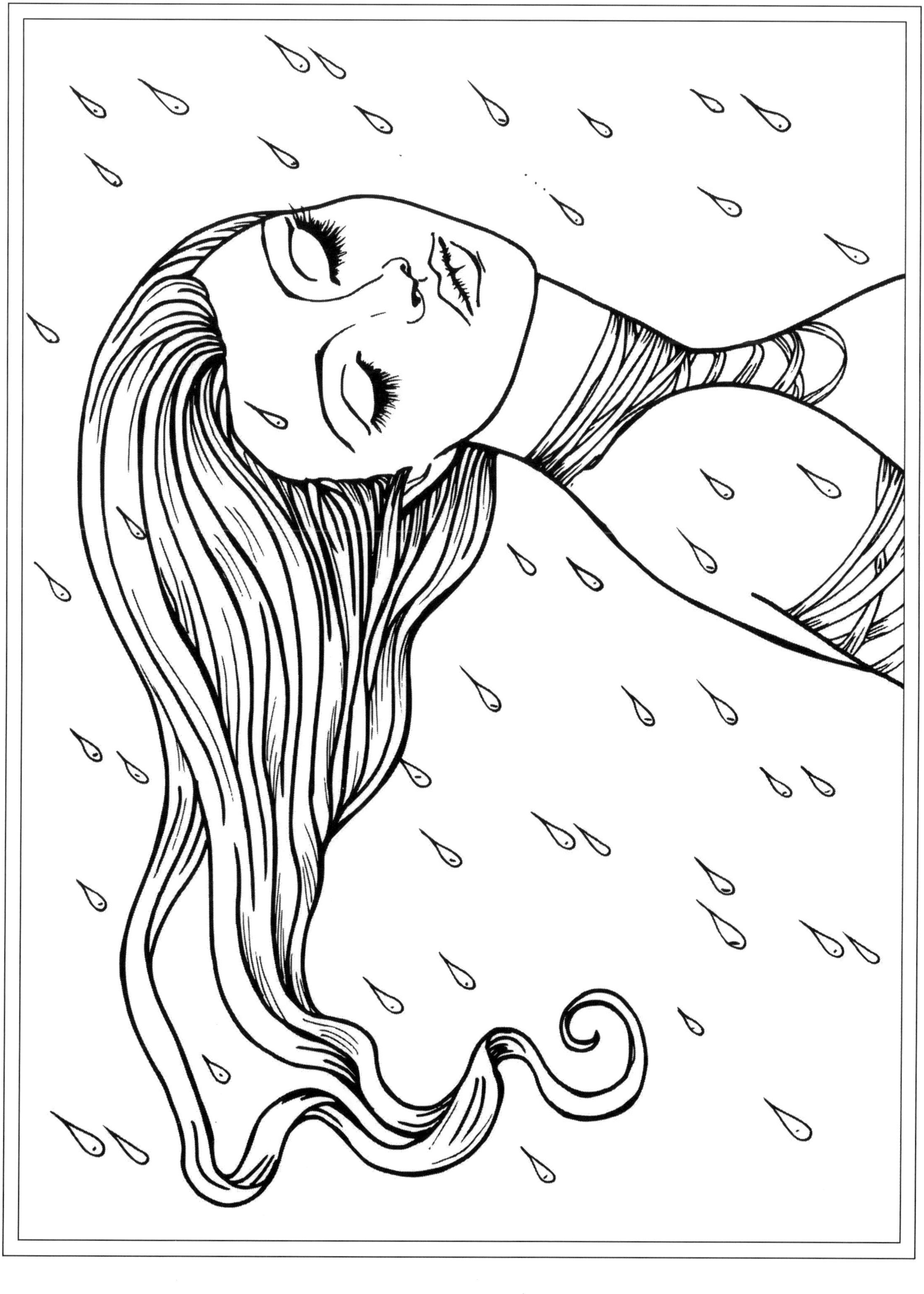

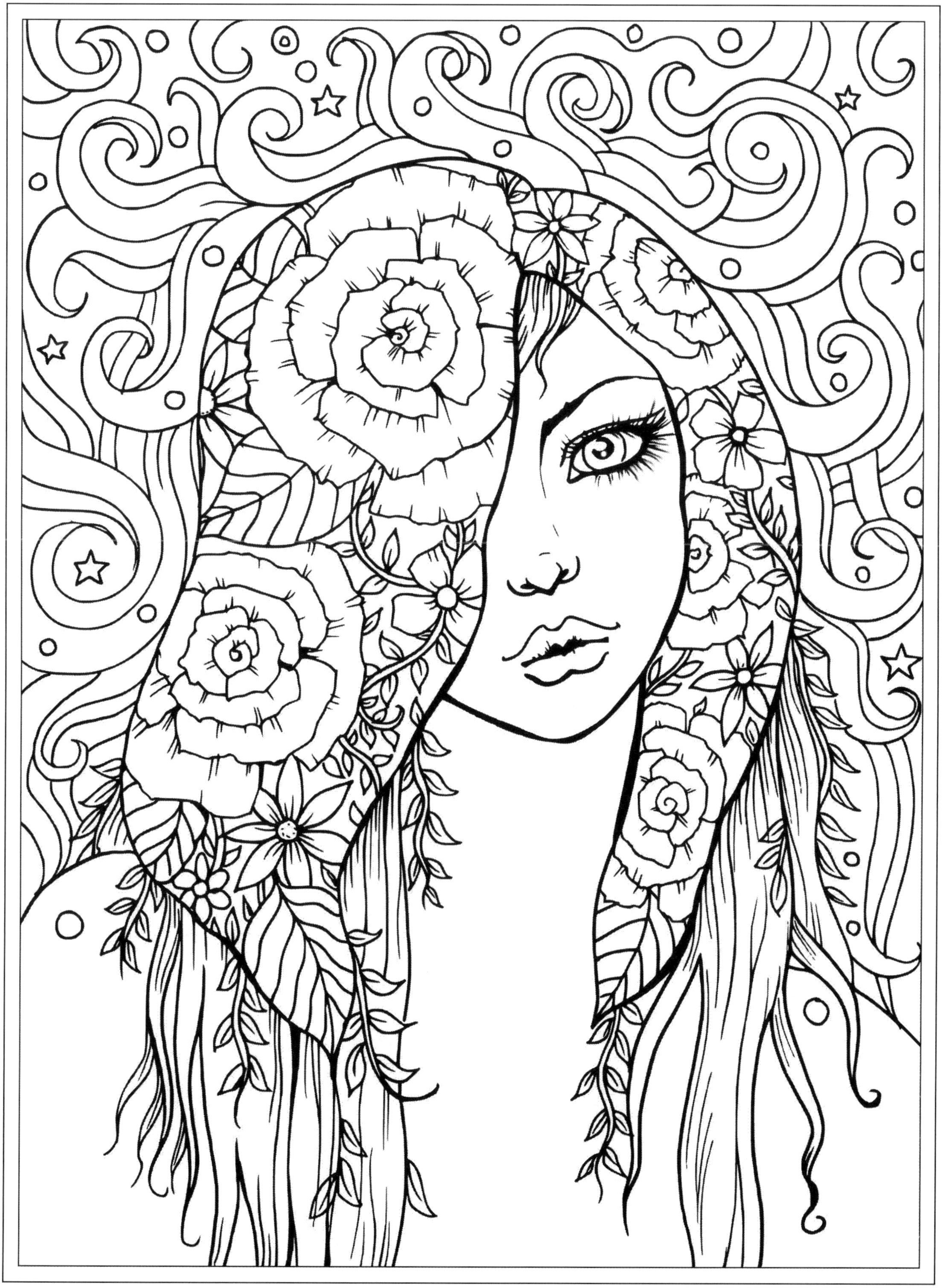

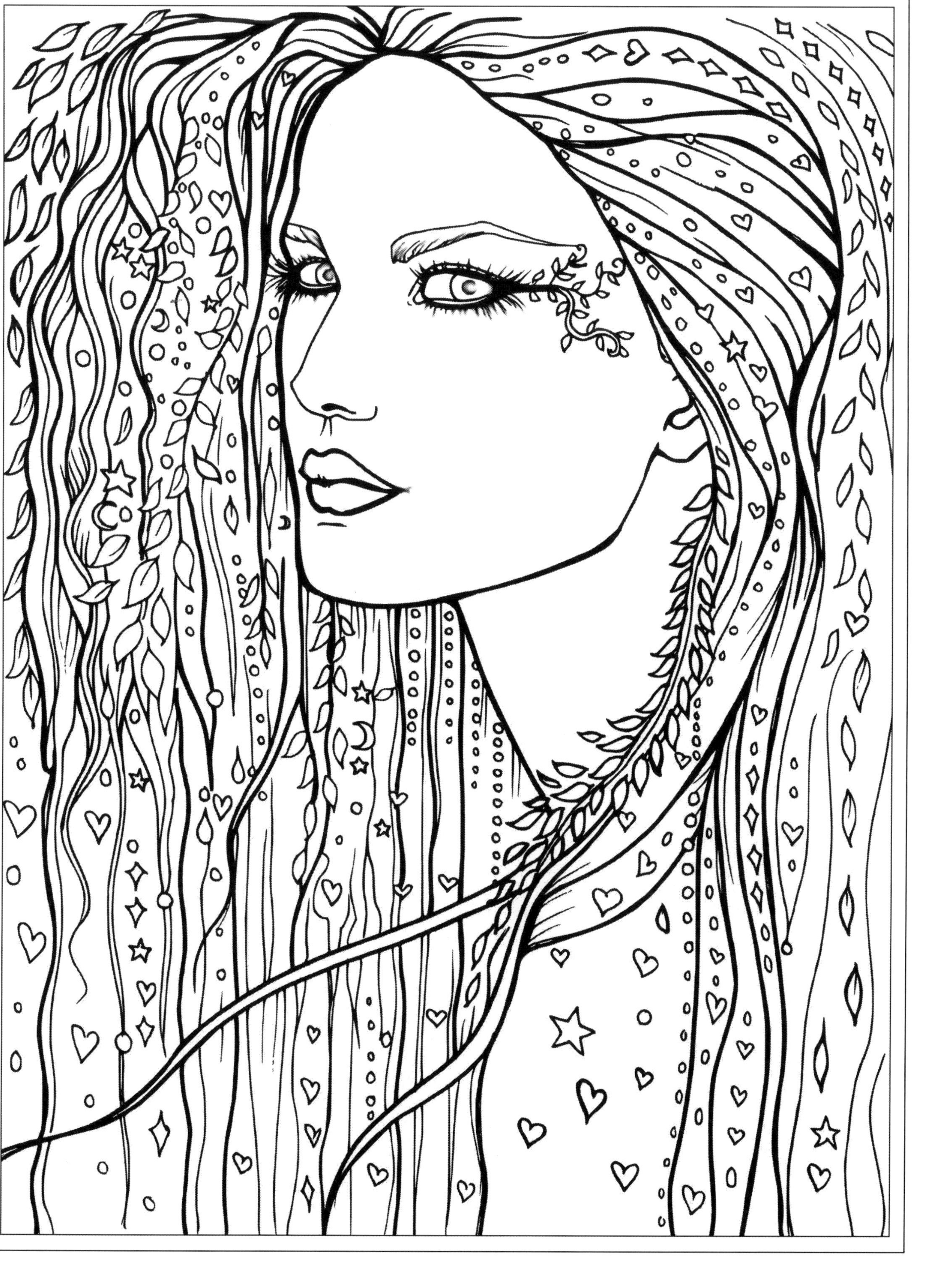

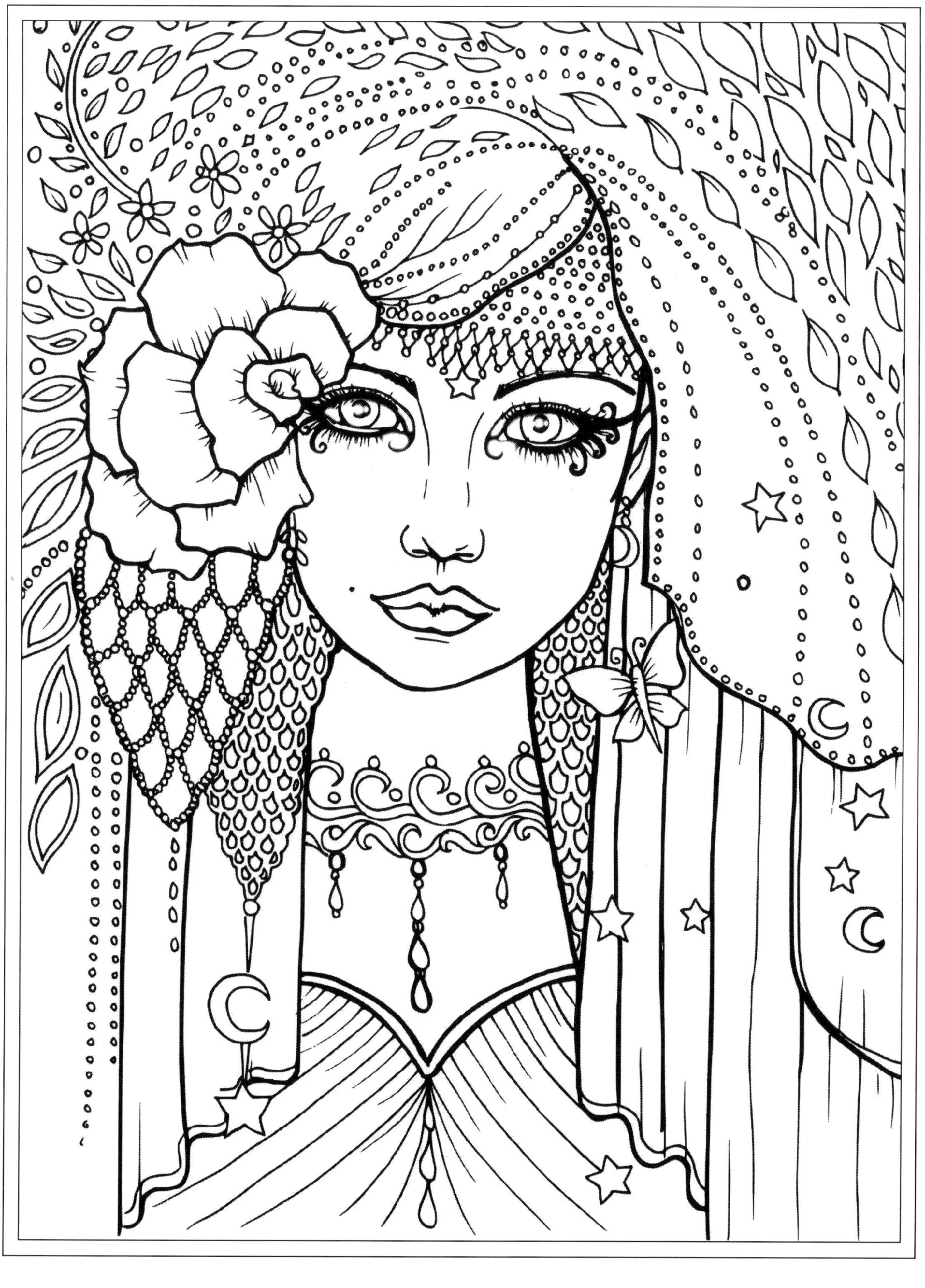

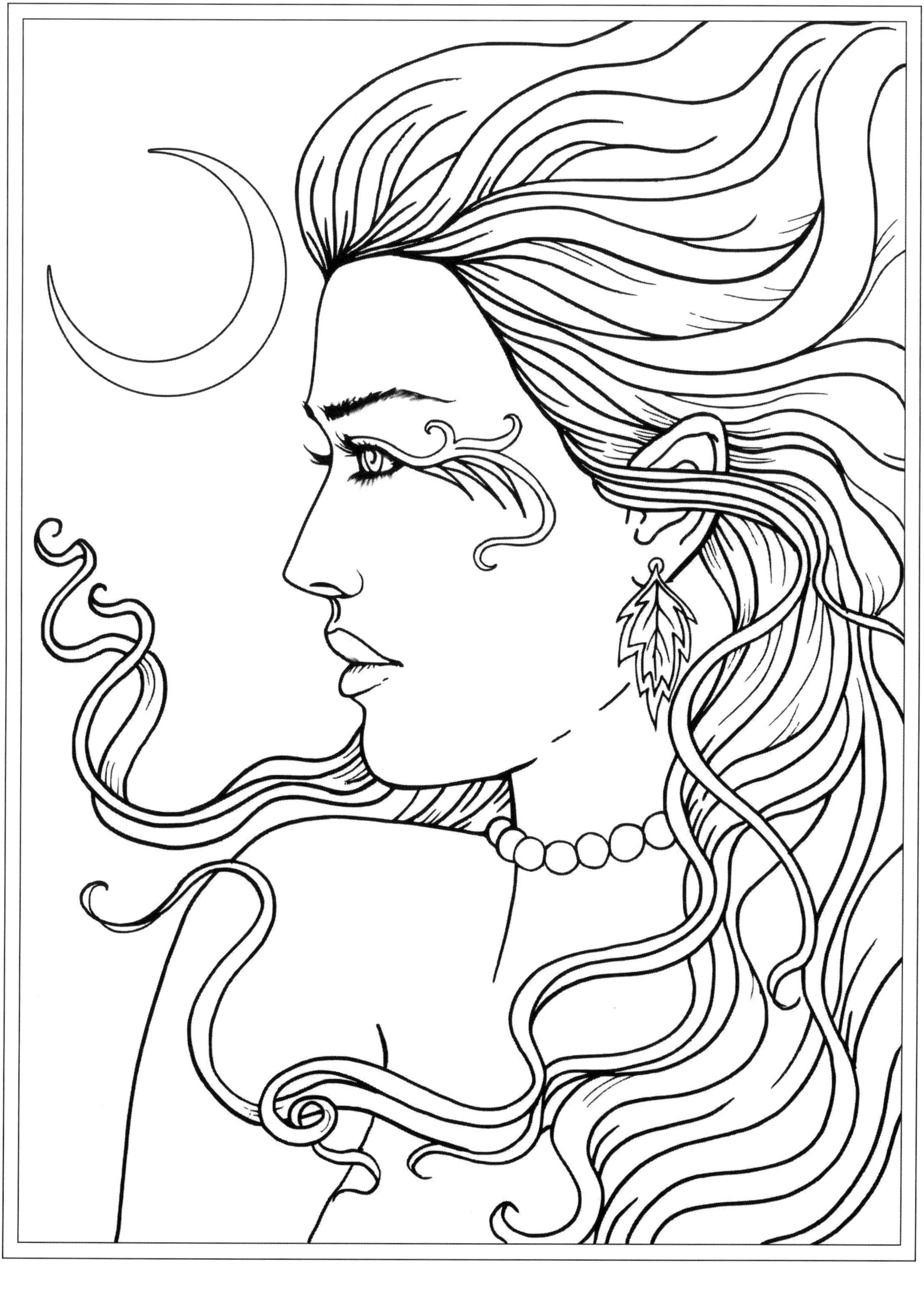

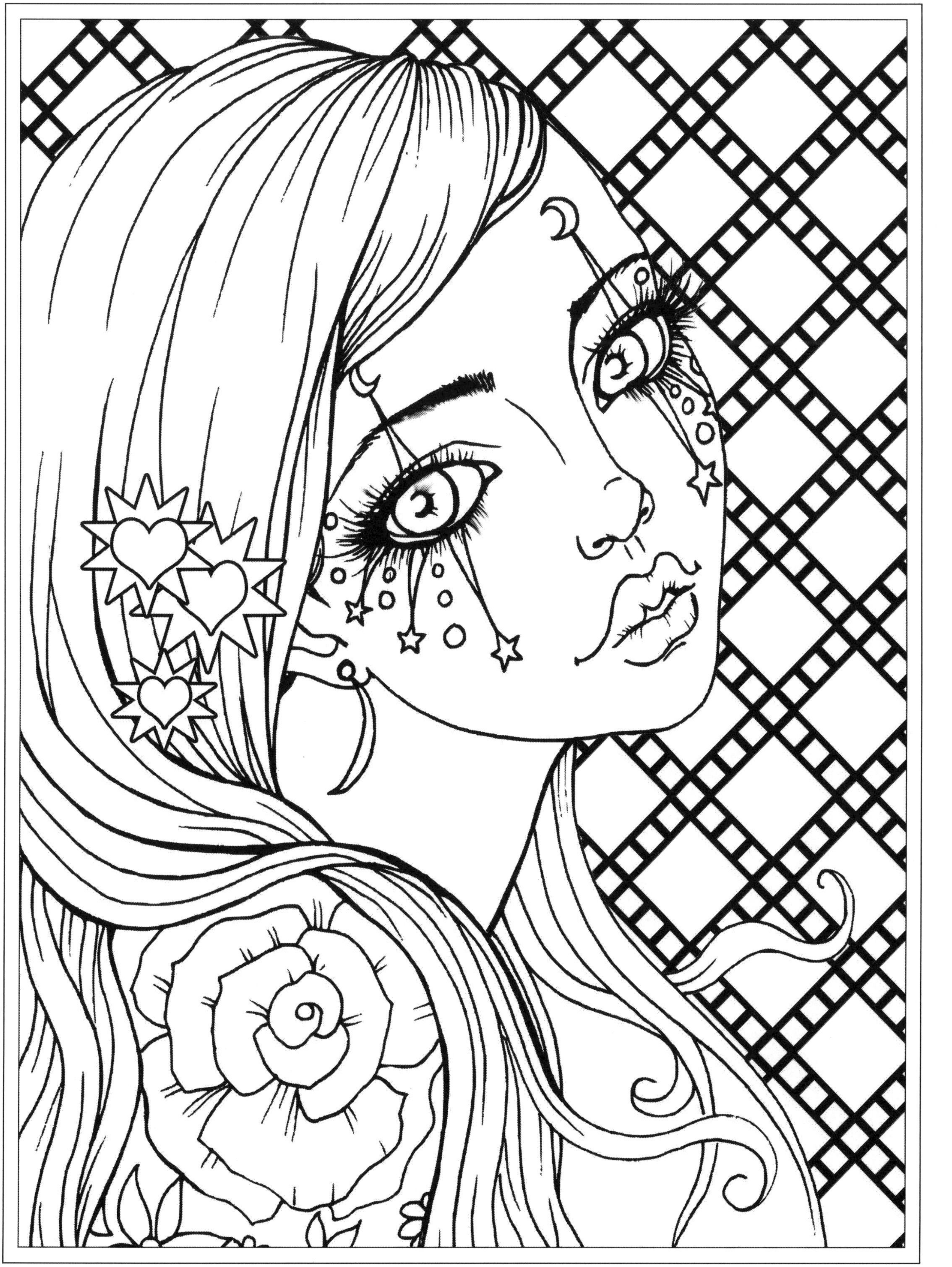

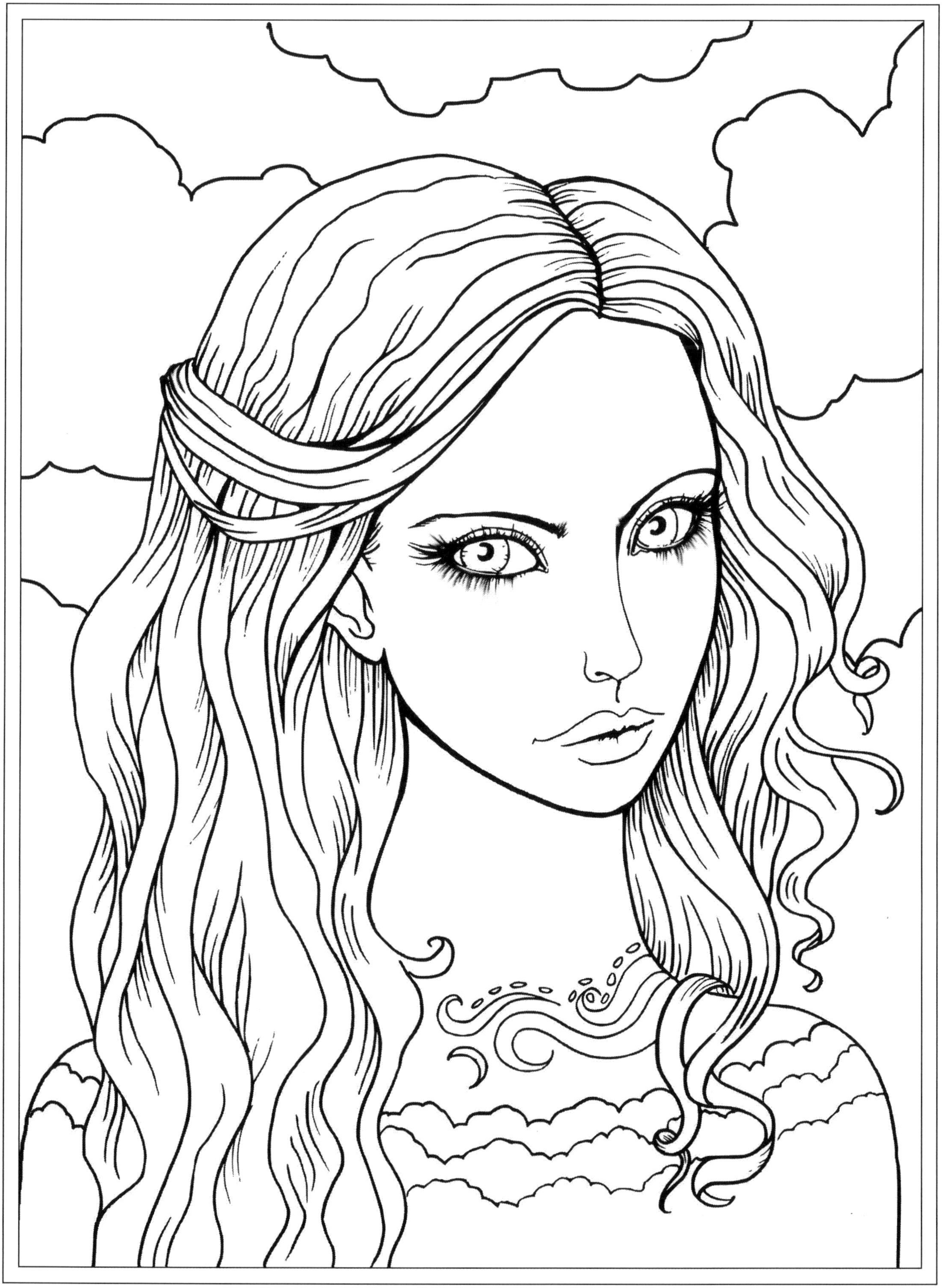

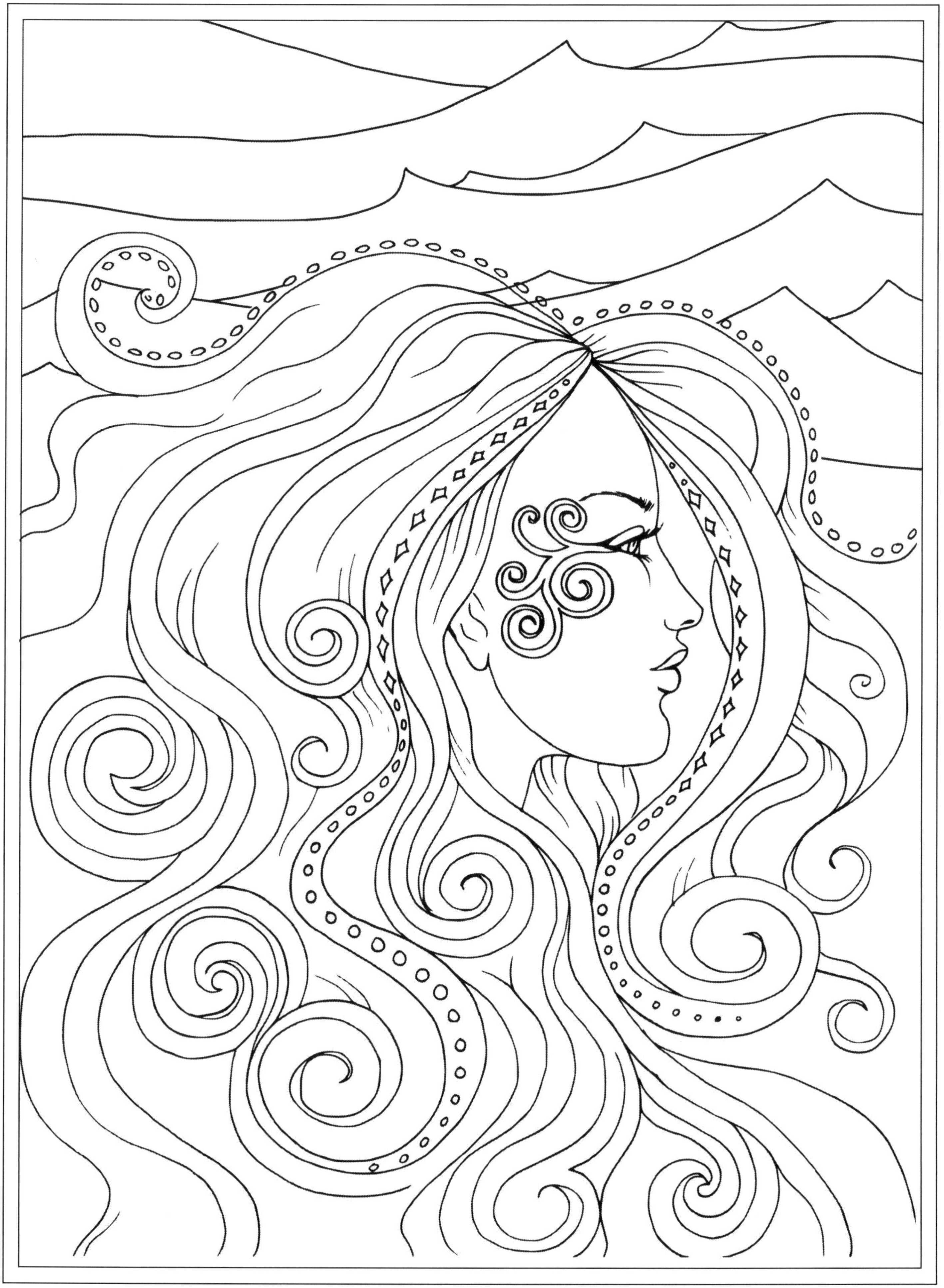

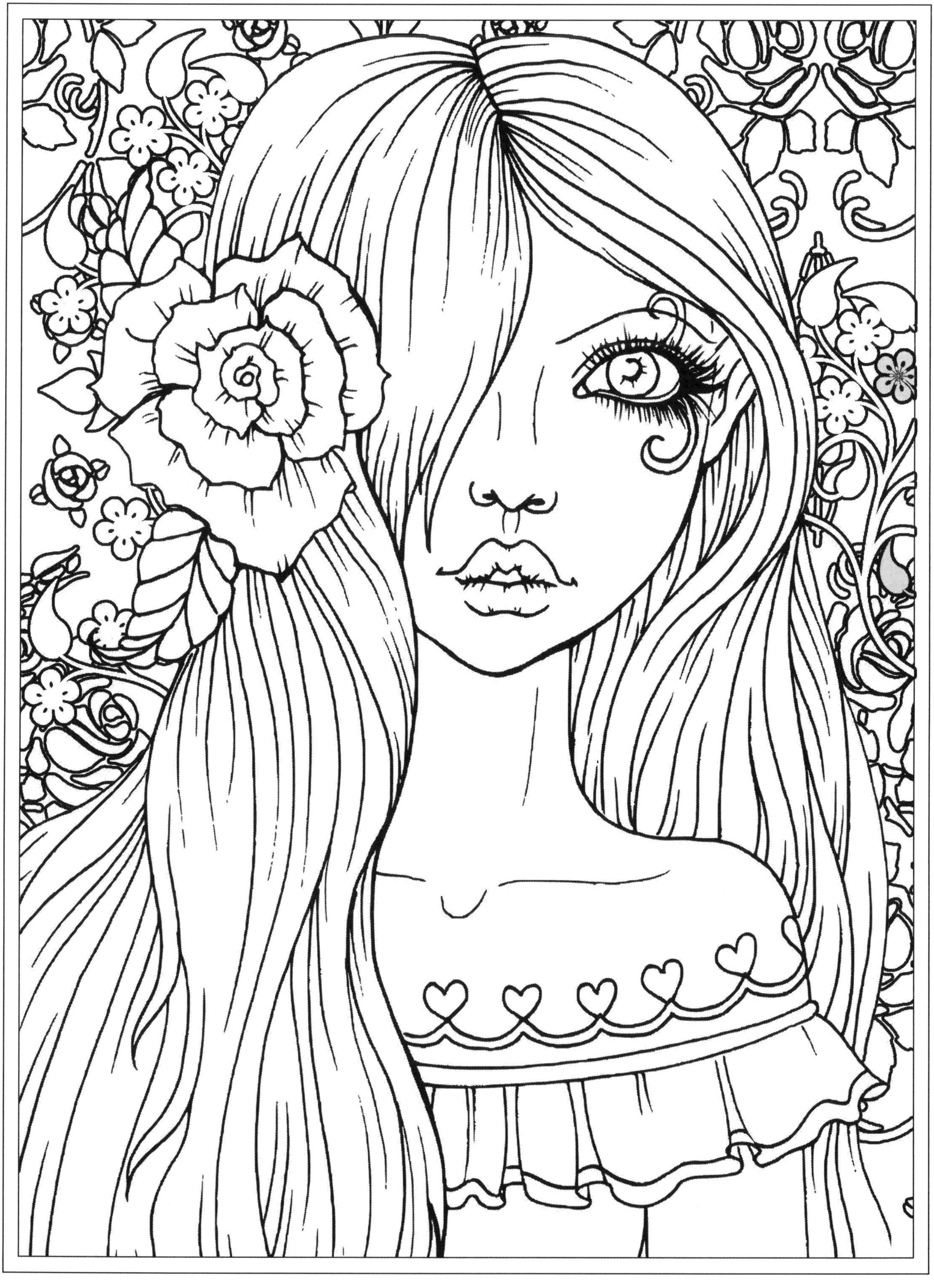

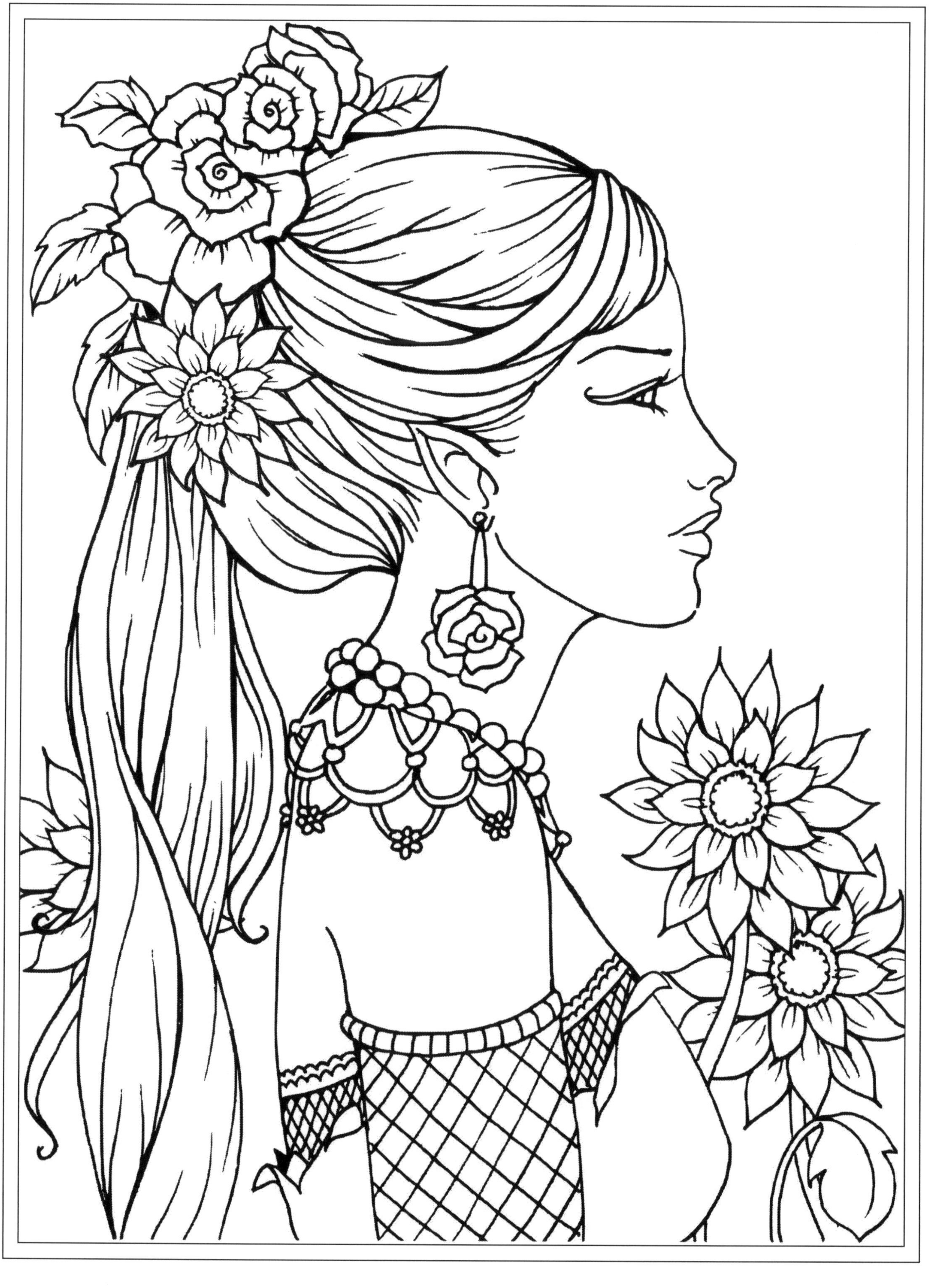

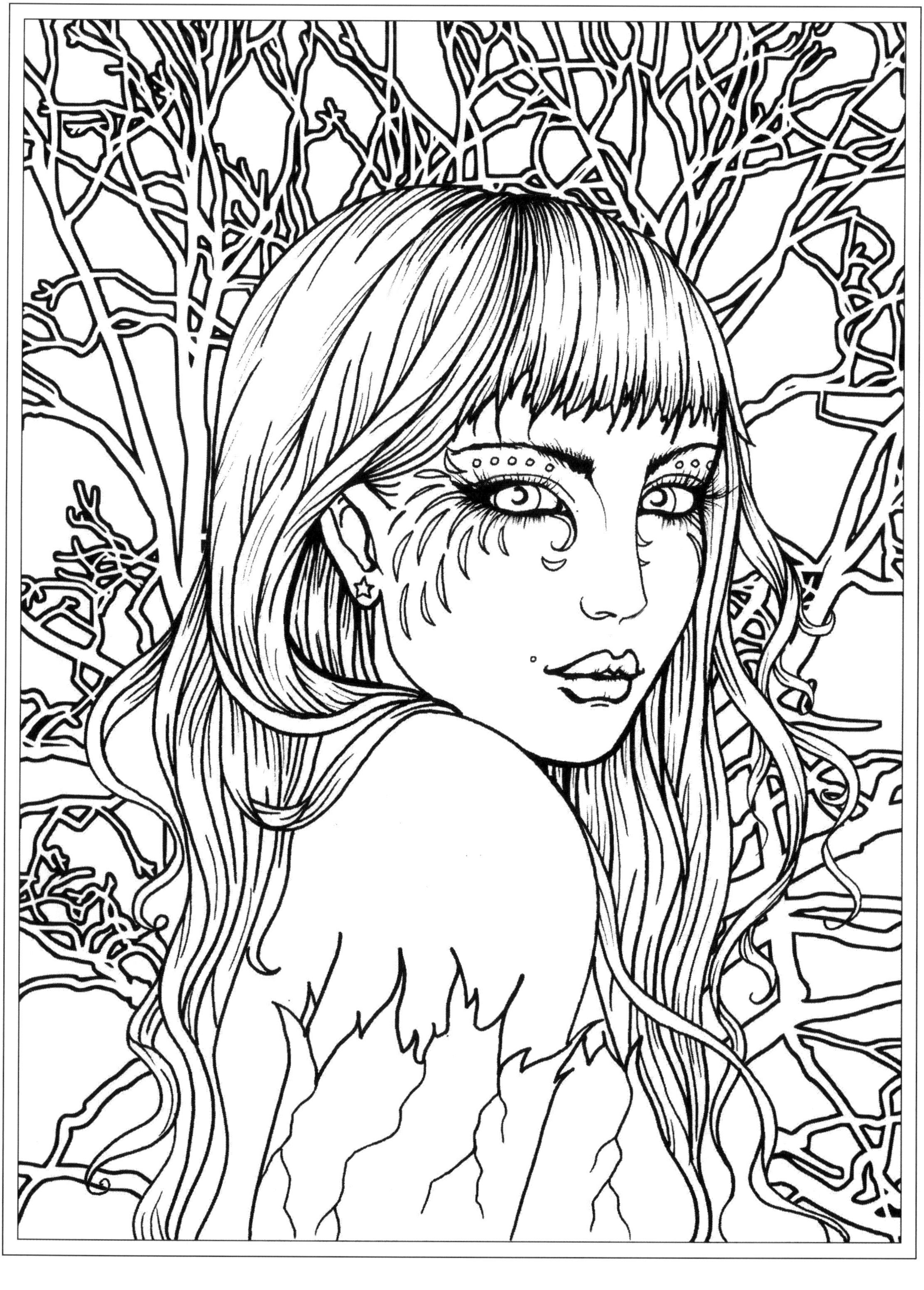

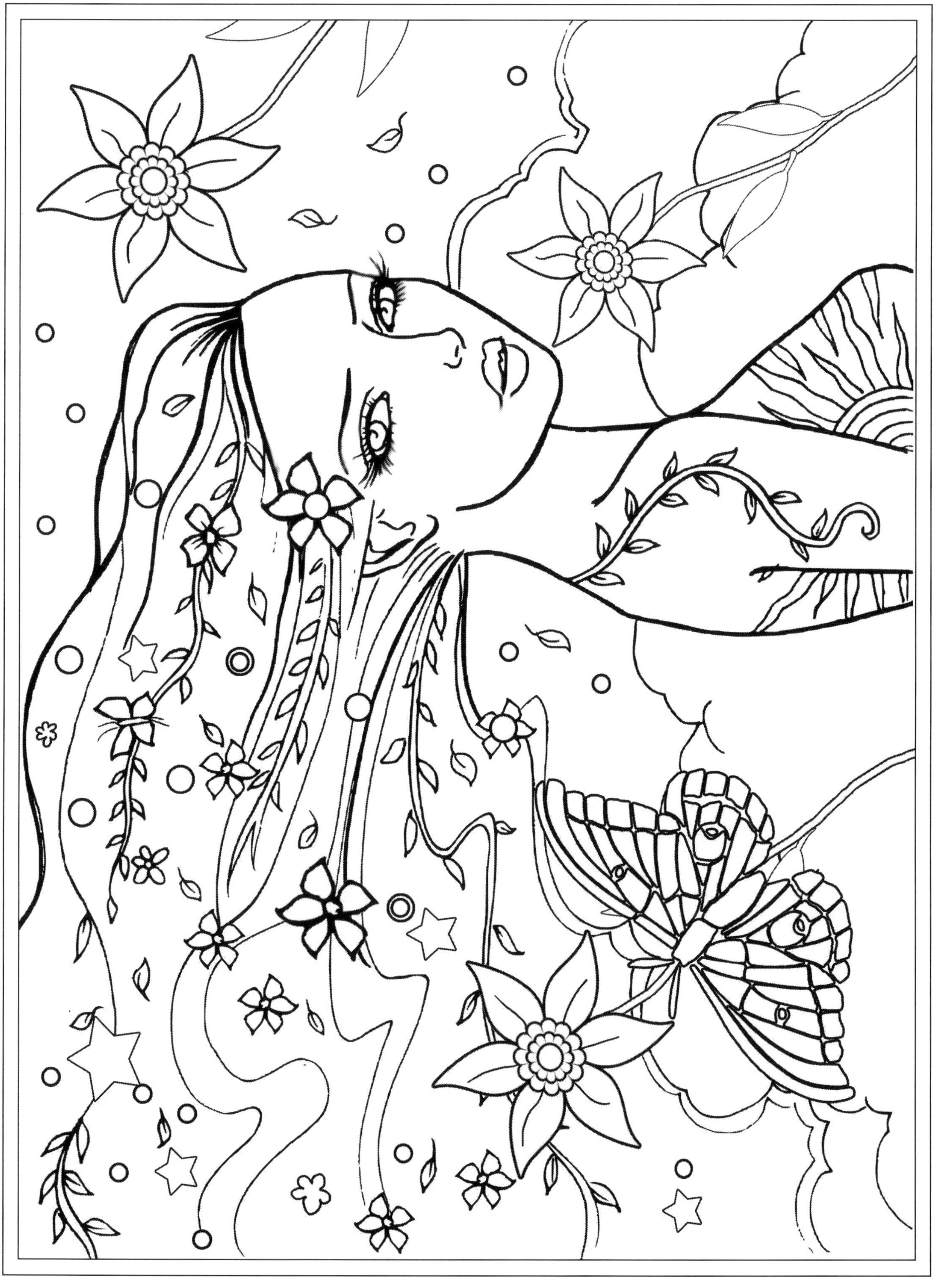

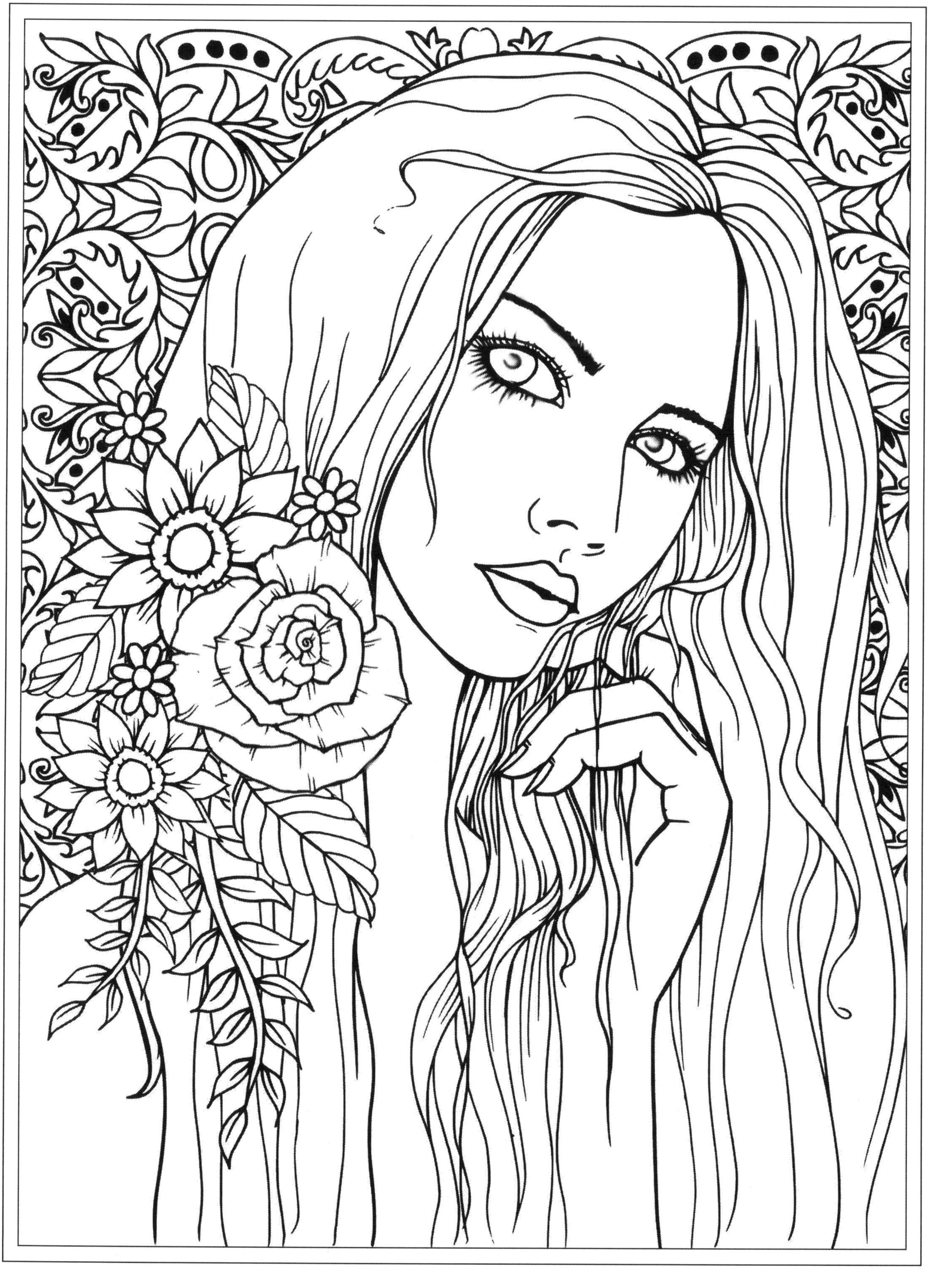

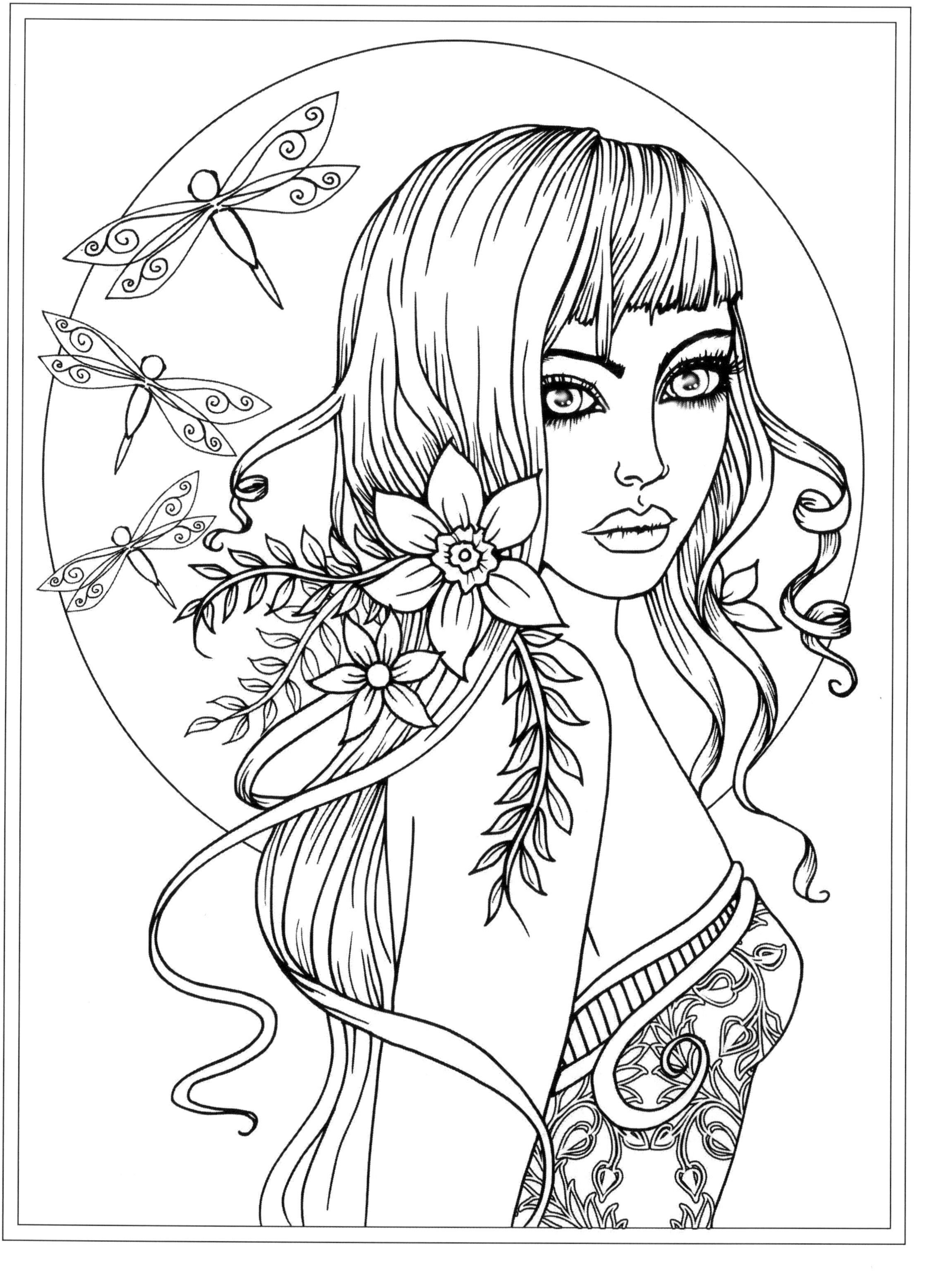

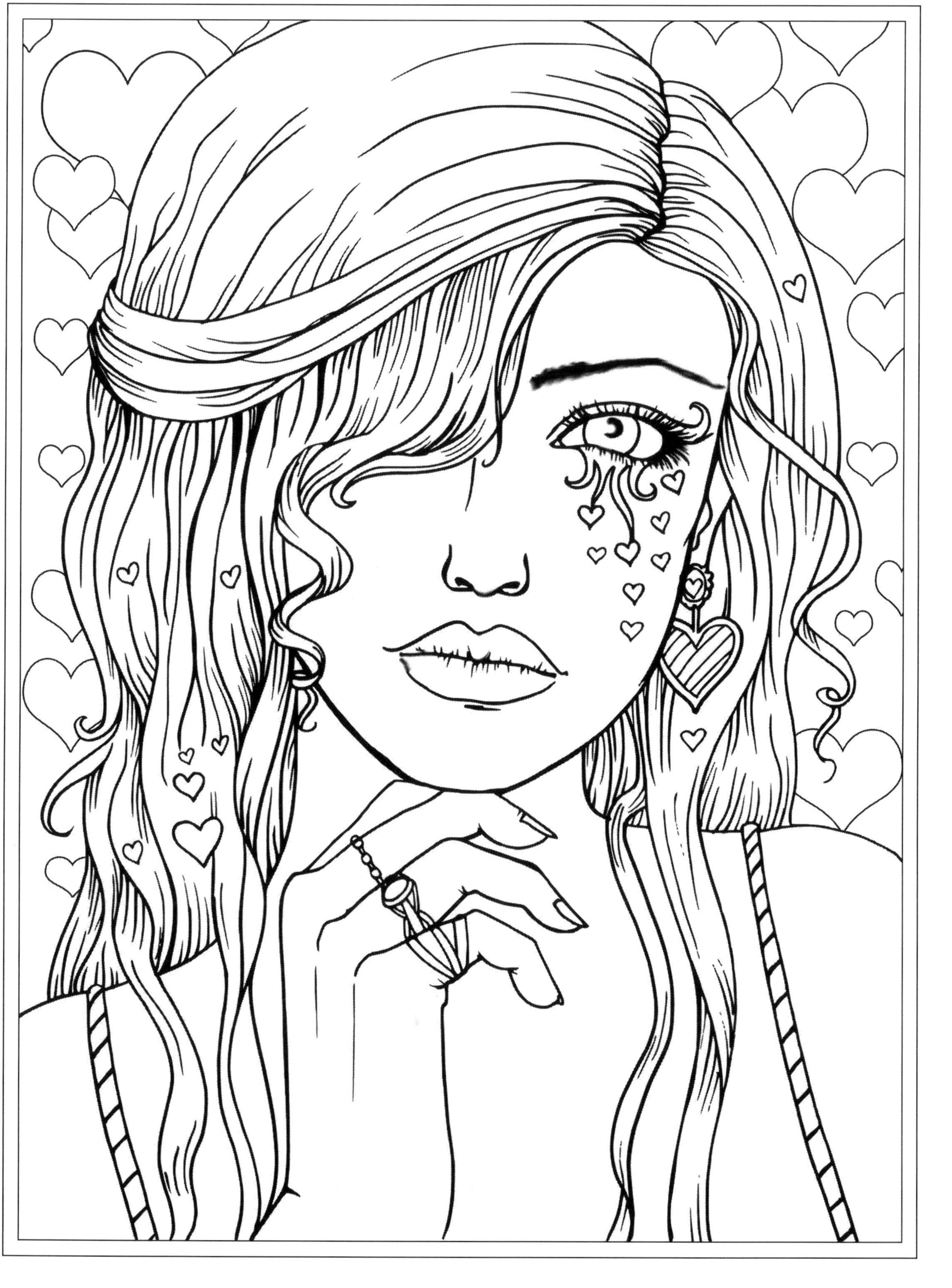

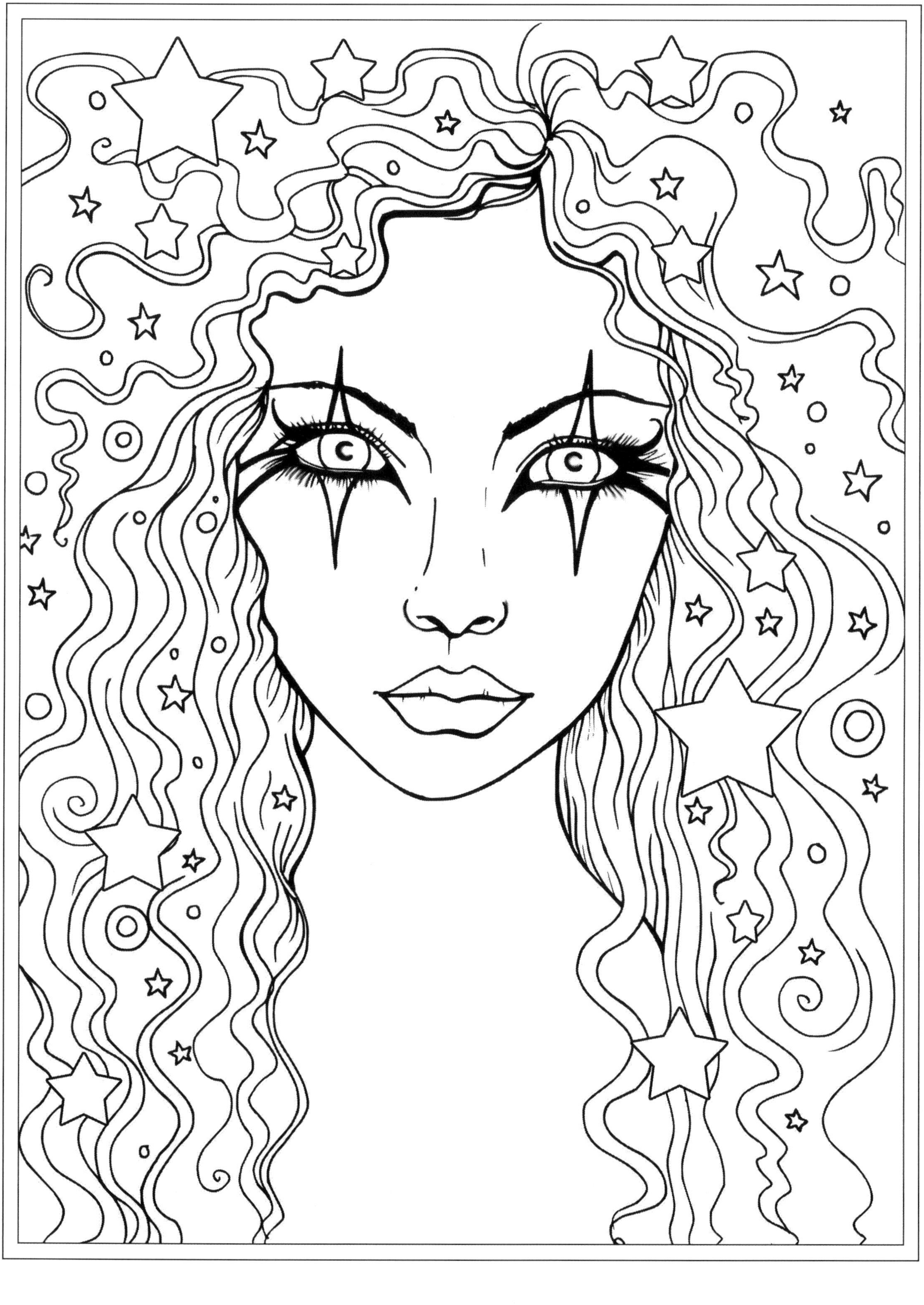

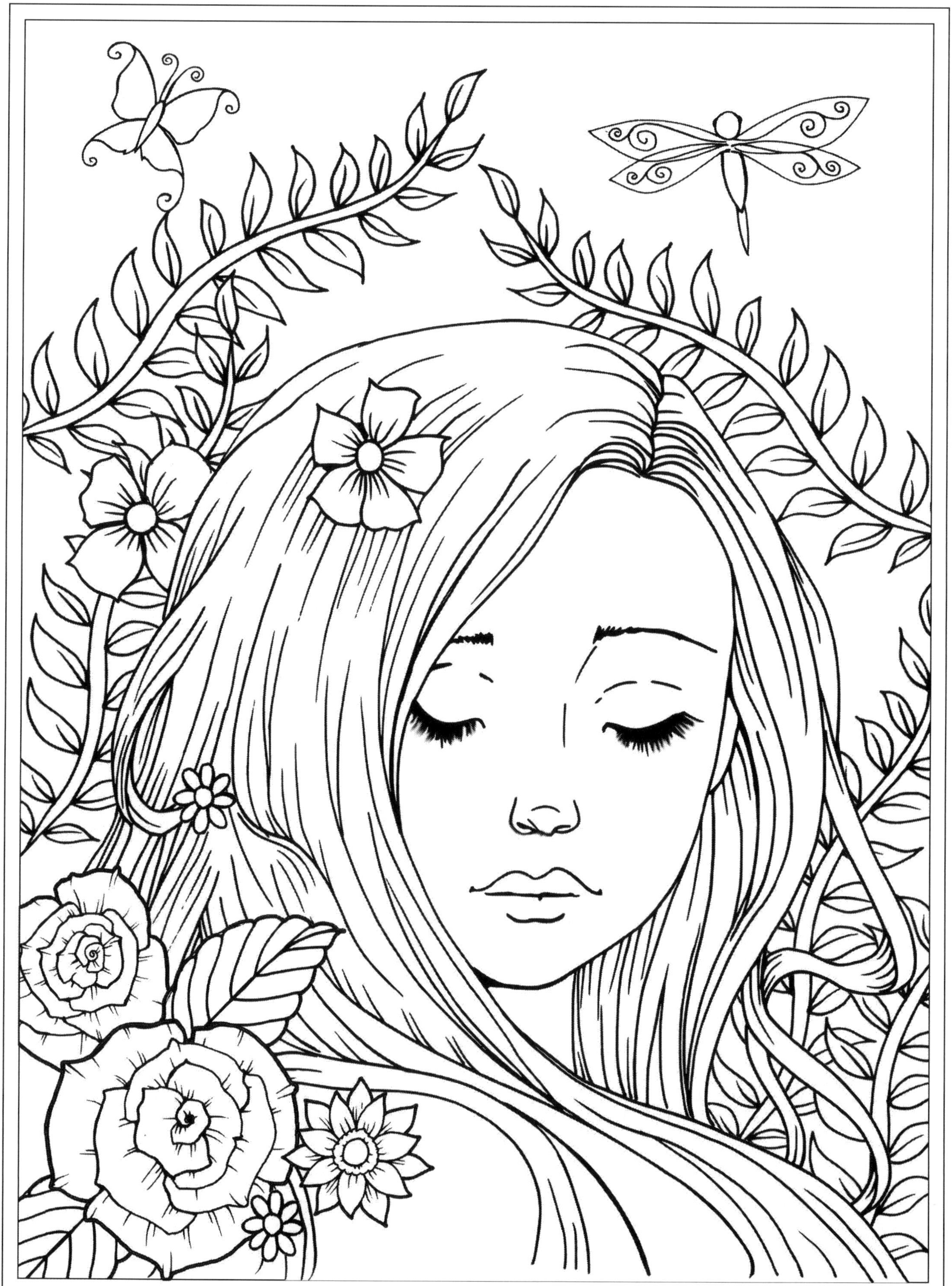

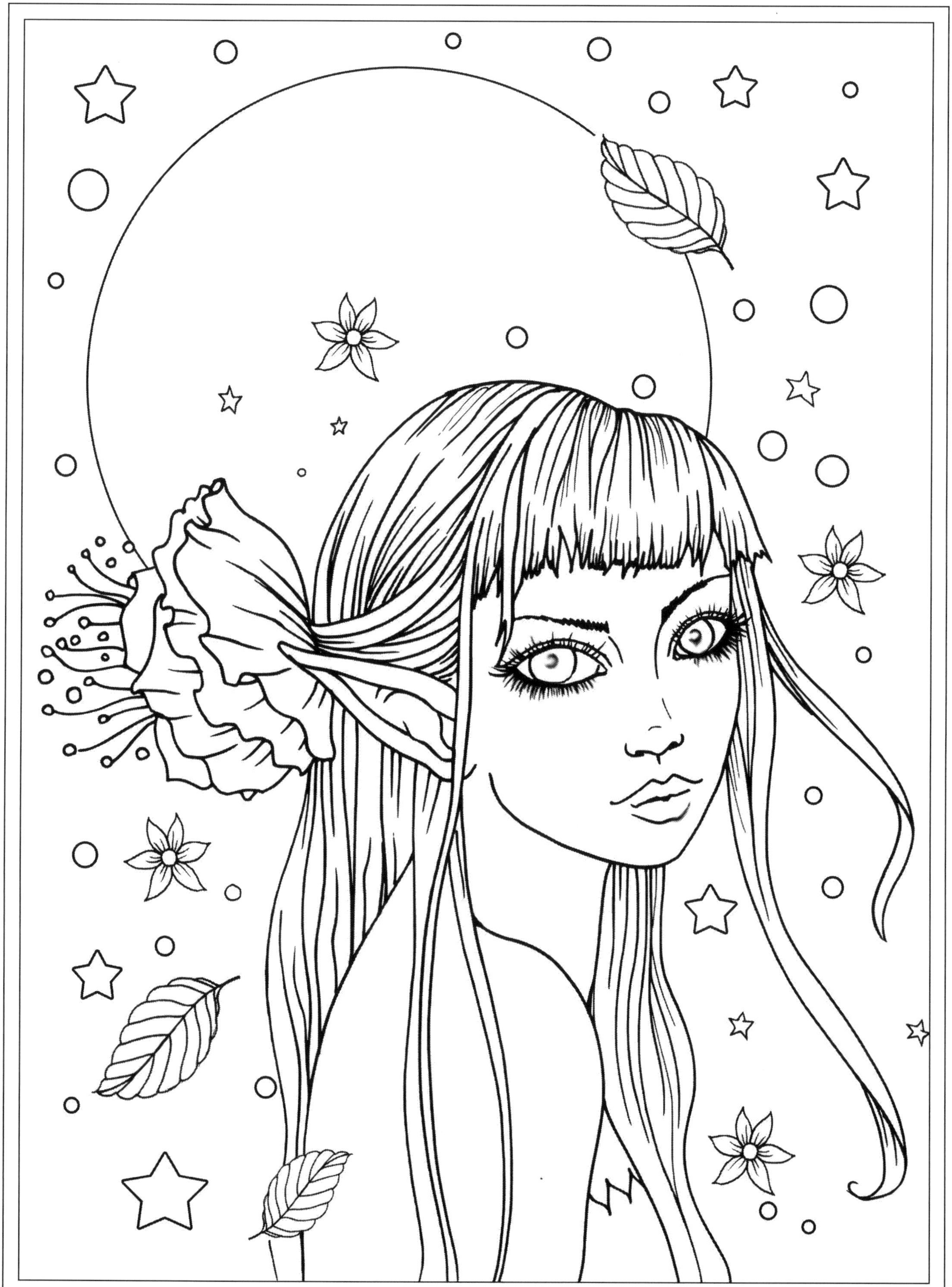

38785739R00031

Made in the USA
Lexington, KY
10 May 2019